THE ULTIMATE RETIREMENT STRATEGY

A GUIDE TO FINANCIAL SECURITY AND FULFILLMENT

Disclaimer

The information provided in this book is for informational purposes only and should not be construed as financial, legal, or tax advice. The strategies and recommendations discussed may not be suitable for everyone. Readers are encouraged to consult with a qualified financial advisor, tax professional, or legal counsel to discuss their specific needs and circumstances. Past performance is not indicative of future results. Investing involves risk, including the potential loss of principal. No strategy or product can guarantee a profit or protect against loss. The author may have a financial interest in the products or services mentioned in this book. Any specific product recommendations are based on the author's professional opinion and may not be suitable for all readers.

Table of Contents

INTRODUCTION

Planning for retirement is a multifaceted process that requires careful consideration of various aspects to ensure financial security and fulfillment. Throughout this book, we will cover critical topics and strategies to help you navigate retirement with confidence:

1. Maximizing Social Security Benefits

2. Creating a Sustainable Income Plan

3. Understanding Sequence of Returns Risk

4. Growth Planning and Asset Allocation

5. Tax Planning for Retirees

6. Healthcare and Long-Term Care Planning

7. Estate Planning Essentials

8. Non-Financial Aspects of Retirement

9. Integrating All Components into a Cohesive Plan

10. Reviewing and Adjusting Your Plan

By taking a proactive approach and implementing the strategies outlined in this book, you can create a retirement plan that provides financial security and enhances your overall well-being.

MAXIMIZING
SOCIAL SECURITY BENEFITS

Overview of Social Security

Social Security is a critical component of most retirees' income, providing a guaranteed source of funds that can help cover essential expenses. Understanding the intricacies of Social Security benefits is essential for maximizing these benefits and enhancing overall retirement planning.

Optimizing Benefits

- **Timing:** One of the most effective strategies for maximizing Social Security benefits is to delay claiming them. While you can start receiving benefits at age 62, waiting until your full retirement age (FRA) or even until age 70 can significantly increase your monthly payments. The increase can be as much as 8% per year for each year you delay past your FRA until age 70.

- ○ **Example:** If your FRA is 66 and your monthly benefit at FRA is $2,000, delaying until age 70 could increase your monthly benefit to $2,640.

- ○ **Detailed Calculation:** Suppose you decide to claim at different ages. Here's how the monthly benefits could look:

  - ▪ **At age 62:** $2,000 - 25% = $1,500 per month

  - ▪ **At age 66:** $2,000 per month

  - ▪ **At age 70:** $2,000 + 32% = $2,640 per month

- **Spousal Benefits:** Married couples have additional strategies available, such as claiming spousal benefits. This can maximize the total benefits received by the couple. The lower-earning spouse can receive up to 50% of the higher-earning spouse's FRA benefit.

  - ○ **Example:** If one spouse's FRA benefit is $2,000, the other spouse can receive up to $1,000 as a spousal benefit.

  - ○ **Detailed Strategy:** The lower-earning spouse might claim spousal benefits at their FRA, while the higher-earning spouse delays their benefits until age 70 to maximize the total household benefit.

- **Earnings Record:** Ensuring that your earnings record is accurate is crucial since Social Security benefits are calculated based on your highest 35 years of earnings.

Reviewing and correcting your earnings record can prevent errors that could reduce your benefits.

- o **How to Review:** Obtain your Social Security Statement annually and verify the recorded earnings. If there are discrepancies, contact the Social Security Administration (SSA) to correct them.

Detailed Explanation of Benefits

Social Security benefits are calculated based on your average indexed monthly earnings (AIME) during the 35 years in which you earned the most. The Social Security Administration (SSA) applies a formula to these earnings to arrive at your primary insurance amount (PIA), which is the amount you'll receive at your full retirement age (FRA).

How Benefits Are Calculated:

1. **AIME Calculation:**
   - o The SSA adjusts your past earnings for inflation.
   - o The highest 35 years of earnings are summed and divided by 420 (the number of months in 35 years) to get the AIME.

2. **PIA Calculation for 2023:**
   - o The SSA applies a formula to your AIME to determine your PIA. For 2023, the formula is:
     - ▪ 90% of the first $1,115 of your AIME

- 32% of your AIME over $1,115 and through $6,721

- 15% of your AIME over $6,721

3. **Full Retirement Age (FRA):**
   - Your FRA depends on your birth year. For those born between 1943 and 1954, the FRA is 66. It gradually increases to 67 for those born in 1960 or later.

Examples of Different Scenarios:

- **Single Individual:** For someone with an AIME of $5,000, the PIA would be calculated as:

  - 90% of $1,115 = $1,003.50

  - 32% of $3,885 ($5,000 - $1,115) = $1,243.20

  - Total PIA = $1,003.50 + $1,243.20 = $2,246.70

- **Married Couple:** Both spouses can receive benefits based on their own earnings records or receive spousal benefits. The lower-earning spouse can receive up to 50% of the higher-earning spouse's PIA.

- **Divorced Individual:** A divorced individual can receive benefits based on their ex-spouse's earnings record if the marriage lasted at least 10 years and they are currently unmarried.

- **Widowed Individual:** A widow or widower can receive benefits based on the deceased spouse's earnings record.

They can begin receiving reduced benefits as early as age 60 or full benefits at their FRA.

Claiming Strategies

Strategies for Singles:

- **Early Claiming:** Benefits can be claimed as early as age 62, but they will be reduced. For example, if your FRA is 66 and you claim at 62, your benefits will be reduced by 25%.

  - **Example:** If your PIA is $2,246.70 at FRA, claiming at 62 would reduce your benefit to approximately $1,685.03.

  - **Detailed Example:** If John decides to claim at 62 instead of 66, he will receive $561.67 less per month ($2,246.70 - $1,685.03).

- **Delayed Claiming:** Benefits increase for each year you delay claiming past your FRA, up to age 70. This can result in an 8% increase per year.

  - **Example:** If your PIA is $2,246.70 at FRA, delaying until age 70 would increase your benefit to approximately $2,956.90.

  - **Detailed Example:** If Mary waits until 70 to claim her benefits, she will receive $710.20 more per month than if she claimed at her FRA ($2,956.90 - $2,246.70).

Strategies for Couples:

- **Widest Split:** Lower wage-earning spouse can file for benefits at FRA, allowing the other spouse to delay their benefits to maximize.

    - **Example:** Susan files for her benefits at 66, allowing her husband tom to delay and maximize his benefits. Tom's benefits continue to grow, and he claims the maximum amount at age 70.

- **Spousal Benefits:** The lower-earning spouse can claim spousal benefits as early as age 62, but they will be reduced if claimed before the higher-earning spouse reaches FRA.

    - **Example:** If one spouse's PIA is $2,246.70, the other spouse can receive up to $1,123.35 as a spousal benefit at FRA. If claimed early, the benefit will be reduced.

    - **Detailed Strategy:** If Susan claims spousal benefits at age 62, she might receive a reduced amount of $842.51 instead of $1,123.35 at her FRA.

Impact of Working While Claiming Benefits:

- **Earnings Limit:** If you claim benefits before your FRA and continue working, your benefits may be reduced if your earnings exceed a certain limit. For 2023, the limit is $21,240. For every $2 earned over the limit, $1 in benefits is withheld.

    - **Example:** If you earn $30,000 in a year while receiving Social Security benefits before FRA, $4,380 of your benefits would be withheld (($30,000 - $21,240) / 2).

- **No Earnings Limit After FRA:** Once you reach your FRA, you can earn any amount without affecting your benefits.

Cost-of-Living Adjustments (COLA):

- Social Security benefits are adjusted annually based on changes in the cost of living. This helps maintain the purchasing power of your benefits over time.

  - **Example:** If the COLA is 2%, a monthly benefit of $2,000 would increase to $2,040 the following year.

Real-Life Case Studies

Case Study 1: Early vs. Delayed Claiming

John, aged 62, decides to claim Social Security benefits early. His FRA is 66, and his benefit at FRA would be $2,246.70 per month. By claiming at 62, his benefit is reduced by 25%, giving him $1,685.03 per month.

Mary, also aged 62, decides to wait until 70 to claim her benefits. Her FRA benefit is also $2,246.70 per month. By waiting, her benefit increases by 8% per year, resulting in a benefit of $2,956.90 per month at age 70.

Scenario:

- John starts receiving benefits immediately, providing him with an earlier income stream but at a lower amount.

- Mary waits and receives a significantly higher monthly benefit, which can be advantageous if she expects to live longer.

Case Study 2: Spousal Benefits

Susan and Tom are a married couple. Tom's FRA benefit is $2,500 per month, while Susan's own FRA benefit is $1,000 per month. Susan decides to claim spousal benefits at FRA, which is 50% of Tom's benefit, giving her $1,250 per month instead of her own benefit.

Scenario:

- Susan benefits from the higher spousal benefit, increasing their combined Social Security income.

- Tom continues working until 70, increasing his benefit to $3,300 per month, and further boosting their overall income.

Common Mistakes to Avoid

1. Claiming Too Early: Many people claim benefits as soon as they are eligible at 62, without considering the long-term reduction in benefits. This can significantly reduce lifetime income.

- **Example:** Claiming at 62 instead of 66 can reduce your benefits by 25% for the rest of your life.

2. Not Reviewing Earnings Record: Errors in your earnings record can lead to lower benefits. It's crucial to review and correct any discrepancies.

- **Tip:** Obtain your Social Security Statement annually and verify the recorded earnings.

3. Ignoring Spousal Benefits: Couples often miss out on maximizing their combined benefits by not coordinating their claiming strategies.

- **Strategy:** Consider strategies like widest split or delayed claiming to maximize household benefits.

4. Not Considering Longevity: Failing to consider life expectancy can result in suboptimal claiming strategies. Delaying benefits can provide a higher income stream if you live longer than expected.

- **Example:** If you expect to live into your 90s, delaying benefits until 70 can provide significantly higher lifetime income.

Visual Aids

Example Chart: Early vs. Delayed Claiming

Age	Monthly Benefit (Claiming at 62)	Monthly Benefit (Claiming at 66)	Monthly Benefit (Claiming at 70)
62	$1,685.03		
66	$1,685.03	$2,246.70	
70	$1,685.03	$2,246.70	$2,956.90

Example Chart: Cumulative Benefits Over Time

Year	John's Cumulative Benefit (Claiming at 62)	Mary's Cumulative Benefit (Claiming at 70)
62	$20,220	
66	$80,160	
70	$141,980	$35,482
75	$242,880	$177,414
80	$344,780	$319,346

Example Table: Combined Social Security Income for Susan and Tom

Age	Monthly Benefit (Claiming at 62)	Monthly Benefit (Claiming at 66)	Monthly Benefit (Claiming at 70)
66	$0	$1,250	$1,250
70	$3,300	$1,250	$4,550
75	$3,300	$1,250	$4,550

Conclusion of Chapter 1

Maximizing Social Security benefits requires a thorough understanding of how benefits are calculated, the impact of claiming age, and the various strategies available. By considering your personal circumstances and coordinating with your spouse, you can optimize your Social Security income and enhance your overall retirement plan. Regularly review your earnings record, stay informed about policy changes, and consult with a financial advisor to ensure you make the best decisions for your financial future.

CHAPTER

TWO

CREATING A SUSTAINABLE INCOME PLAN

Importance of Income Planning

A sustainable income plan ensures that retirees have enough money to cover their expenses throughout retirement. It's crucial to balance income sources to manage longevity risk and maintain financial stability. Income planning involves understanding your expenses, projecting future costs, and identifying reliable income sources.

The Bucket Plan® Approach

The Bucket Plan® segments retirement assets into different "buckets" based on time horizons:

1. **Short-Term Bucket:** Cash and low-risk investments for immediate needs (0-1 years).

2. **Intermediate Bucket:** Income for the next 10 years.

3. **Long-Term Bucket:** Growth-oriented investments for long-term needs (10+ years).

Example Allocation:

- **Short-Term Bucket:** $50,000 in cash and short-term bonds for the first year of retirement.

- **Intermediate Bucket:** $500,000 in a mix of bonds and dividend-paying stocks or FIAs for years 2-10.

- **Long-Term Bucket:** $500,000 in growth-oriented investments, including stocks and real estate, for years 10+.

Strategies for Ensuring Income Longevity

1. Guaranteed Income Sources:

- **Pensions:** Regular payments from employer-sponsored pension plans.

- **Annuities:** Financial products that provide a guaranteed income stream, such as fixed annuities and fixed indexed annuities.

  - **Fixed Annuities:** Provide a guaranteed payout that does not change over time.

  - **Fixed Indexed Annuities:** Offer potential for higher payouts linked to market performance, while still providing a guaranteed minimum with no risk of loss.

2. Dynamic Withdrawal Strategies:

- Adjust withdrawals based on market performance and personal circumstances.

- **Example:** The Guyton-Klinger Rule, which allows for flexible withdrawals based on market conditions and spending needs.

  - Implementation: In good market years, withdraw a higher percentage; in bad market years, reduce withdrawals to preserve capital.

3. Spending Prioritization:

- Differentiate between essential and discretionary expenses.

- Ensure essential expenses are covered by guaranteed income sources.

- **Budgeting Tips:** Track your expenses, categorize them into needs and wants, and adjust your spending plan accordingly.

4. Rebalancing the Portfolio:

- Regularly rebalance your portfolio to maintain your desired asset allocation.

- **Example:** If the equity portion of your portfolio grows significantly, sell some equities and buy bonds to maintain balance.

- **Frequency:** Consider rebalancing annually or when the allocation deviates by a certain percentage.

Case Studies and Examples

Case Study 1: Using the Bucket Plan® to Balance Risk and Income Needs

John and Mary are a married couple entering retirement. They have $1 million in savings and need a sustainable income plan. They decide to use the Bucket Plan® approach.

Scenario:

- **Short-Term Bucket:** $50,000 in cash and short-term bonds for the first year of retirement.

- **Intermediate Bucket:** $450,000 in a mix of bonds and dividend-paying stocks or FIAs for years 2-10.

- **Long-Term Bucket:** $500,000 in growth-oriented investments, including stocks and real estate, for years 10+.

Outcome:

- In the first 5 years, John and Mary rely on the short-term bucket for their living expenses, avoiding the need to sell investments during market downturns.

- As they approach year 5, they start drawing from the intermediate bucket, allowing their long-term investments to continue growing.

Case Study 2: Managing Withdrawals During Market Fluctuations to Preserve Capital

Susan is a single retiree with $800,000 in retirement savings. She plans to withdraw 4% annually but wants to avoid depleting her savings during market downturns.

Strategy:

- Susan adopts a dynamic withdrawal strategy, adjusting her withdrawals based on market performance.

- During good market years, she withdraws 4% of her portfolio's value.

- During bad market years, she reduces her withdrawals to 3% to preserve capital.

Outcome:

- In a year when the market returns 10%, Susan withdraws $32,000 (4% of $800,000).

- In a year when the market drops 10%, she withdraws $21,600 (3% of $720,000, the reduced portfolio value).

Case Study 3: Utilizing Fixed Indexed Annuities for Guaranteed Income

Tom and Lisa are concerned about market volatility affecting their retirement income. They decide to allocate a portion of their savings to fixed indexed annuities.

Strategy:

- Tom and Lisa invest $300,000 in fixed indexed annuities, which provide a guaranteed minimum income and potential for higher payouts based on market performance.

Outcome:

- They receive a guaranteed monthly income from the annuities, providing financial security and peace of mind.

- The potential for higher payouts allows them to benefit from market gains without risking their principal.

Common Mistakes to Avoid

1. **Overestimating Investment Returns:** Assuming high returns can lead to overspending and depletion of savings. It's important to use conservative estimates.

   - **Example:** Planning based on an average return of 4-5% instead of 7-8% can provide a more realistic picture.

2. Underestimating Expenses: Failing to account for healthcare costs, inflation, and lifestyle changes can result in inadequate savings.

   - **Tip:** Regularly review and update your budget to reflect changes in expenses.

3. **Ignoring Tax Implications:** Withdrawals from tax-deferred accounts are subject to income tax. Understanding the tax impact can help in planning efficient withdrawals.

- o **Example:** Plan to withdraw from taxable accounts first, then tax-deferred accounts, and lastly, tax-free accounts like Roth IRAs.

4. **Neglecting Rebalancing:** Regularly rebalancing your portfolio ensures that your asset allocation remains aligned with your risk tolerance and investment goals.

   - o **Tip:** Set a specific threshold (e.g., 5%) for when to rebalance your portfolio.

Visual Aids

Example Chart: The Bucket Plan® Allocation

Bucket Type	Time Horizon	Investment Type	Allocation Amount
Short-Term Bucket	0-1 years	Cash, Short-term Bonds	$200,000
Intermediate Bucket	2-10 years	Bonds, Dividends Stocks, FIA's	$300,000
Long-Term Bucket	10+ years	Growth Oriented Investments	$500,000

Example Chart: Dynamic Withdrawal Strategy

Year	Market Return	Portfolio Value	Withdrawal Percentage	Withdrawal Amount
1	+10%	$800,000	4%	$32,000
2	-10%	$720,000	3%	$21,600
3	+5%	$756,000	4%	$30,240
4	0%	$756,000	4%	$30,240

Example Table: Fixed Indexed Annuities Benefits

Feature	Description
Guaranteed Minimum Income	Provides a fixed monthly income regardless of market performance
Market – Linked Growth	Potential for higher income based on market index performance
Principal Protection	Protects the initial investment from market losses

Conclusion of Chapter 2

Creating a sustainable income plan is essential for ensuring that you have enough money to cover your expenses throughout retirement. By using strategies like the Bucket Plan®, dynamic withdrawals, and fixed indexed annuities, you can manage risk, preserve capital, and maintain financial stability. Understanding your expenses, projecting future costs, and identifying reliable income sources are key steps in achieving a secure and fulfilling retirement.

CHAPTER

THREE

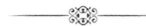

UNDERSTANDING
SEQUENCE OF RETURNS RISK

Definition and Explanation

Sequence of returns risk refers to the risk that the timing of withdrawals from retirement accounts will negatively impact the overall value of the portfolio. This risk is not about the average rate of return over time but the specific order in which returns occur. When withdrawals are made during market downturns, it can deplete retirement savings faster because there is less capital left to recover when the market rebounds. This risk is particularly critical during the early years of retirement when negative returns can have a more significant impact.

Impact on Retirement Savings

The impact of sequence of returns risk on retirement savings can be profound. For example, if you retire during a market downturn and start withdrawing from your investments, the withdrawals can compound the losses and reduce your portfolio's value significantly. This can lead to a situation where your savings are depleted faster than expected, even if the market eventually recovers.

Detailed Example:

- **Scenario A:** Retiree A begins retirement with $1 million and withdraws $50,000 annually. In the first three years, the market returns are -10%, -10%, and +15%. After three years, Retiree A's portfolio might be significantly lower than expected.

- **Scenario B:** Retiree B also begins with $1 million and withdraws $50,000 annually. In the first three years, the market returns are +15%, -10%, and -10%. Retiree B's portfolio is in a better position despite having the same average return as Retiree A.

Case Studies and Examples

Case Study 1: Retiree A vs. Retiree B

Retiree A and Retiree B both start retirement with $1 million in savings. Retiree A retires in a year when the market drops 20%, while Retiree B retires in a year when the market gains 20%. Despite having identical portfolios, Retiree A might have to withdraw a larger percentage of their diminished portfolio, leading to quicker depletion of funds.

Scenario:

- **Retiree A:** Starts withdrawing $50,000 annually in a year when the portfolio drops by 20% to $800,000. After the first year, the portfolio is $750,000 (after withdrawal).

- **Retiree B:** Starts withdrawing $50,000 annually in a year when the portfolio increases by 20% to $1.2 million. After the first year, the portfolio is $1.15 million (after withdrawal).

Outcome:

- Retiree A's portfolio continues to shrink more rapidly due to initial losses and ongoing withdrawals.

- Retiree B's portfolio remains more robust despite identical withdrawal rates and market returns over time.

Visual Aid:

- A comparison chart illustrating the different trajectories of Retiree A and Retiree B's portfolios over time.

Case Study 2: Historical Data Analysis

Comparing historical data, such as the impact on retirees who started withdrawing during the 2008 financial crisis versus those who began in the mid-1990s bull market, can illustrate the significant differences in outcomes due to sequence of returns.

Scenario:

- **2008 Retiree:** Begins withdrawing during a severe market downturn, significantly impacting the portfolio's ability to recover.

- **1990s Retiree:** Begins withdrawing during a prolonged market upswing, allowing the portfolio to grow even with regular withdrawals.

Outcome:

- The 2008 retiree's portfolio may struggle to recover, leading to reduced longevity of their savings.

- The 1990s retiree benefits from market growth, enhancing the sustainability of their withdrawals.

Mitigation Strategies

1. Diversification:

- Spread investments across various asset classes to reduce exposure to any single asset's poor performance.

- **Example:** Include a mix of stocks, bonds, real estate, and other assets in your portfolio to balance risk.

2. Dynamic Withdrawal Strategies:

- Adjusting withdrawal rates based on market performance can help preserve capital.

- **Example:** The Guyton-Klinger Rule allows for flexible withdrawals based on market conditions, reducing withdrawals in bad years and increasing them in good years.

3. Buffer Assets:

- Maintaining a reserve of low-risk assets, such as cash or short-term bonds, to draw from during market downturns.

- **Example:** Keep 2-3 years of living expenses in cash or short-term bonds to avoid selling investments at a loss.

4. Annuities:

- Providing a guaranteed income stream unaffected by market fluctuations. Fixed indexed annuities, for example, can offer growth potential while protecting against downside risk.

- **Example:** Allocate a portion of your portfolio to annuities to ensure a steady income regardless of market conditions.

5. Rebalancing:

- Regularly rebalance your portfolio to maintain the desired asset allocation and manage risk.

- **Example:** If the equity portion of your portfolio grows significantly, sell some equities and buy bonds to restore balance.

Detailed Example:

Scenario:

- Retiree A uses a dynamic withdrawal strategy and reduces their withdrawal rate during the first three years of a market downturn.

- Retiree B maintains a fixed withdrawal rate regardless of market conditions.

Outcome:

- Retiree A's portfolio recovers more effectively, sustaining their withdrawals longer.

- Retiree B's portfolio depletes faster due to the fixed withdrawal rate during downturns.

Common Mistakes to Avoid

1. Not Having a Buffer: Failing to maintain a reserve of low-risk assets can force you to sell investments at a loss during market downturns.

- **Tip:** Keep 2-3 years of living expenses in a cash reserve to weather market downturns.

2. Ignoring Sequence of Returns Risk: Overlooking the importance of the order of returns can lead to underestimating the risk to your portfolio.

- **Example:** Retirees who begin withdrawals during a market downturn can see their portfolios deplete faster than those who start during a market upswing.

3. Static Withdrawal Rates: Rigidly sticking to a fixed withdrawal rate regardless of market conditions can accelerate the depletion of your savings.

- **Tip:** Consider dynamic withdrawal strategies that adjust based on market performance.

4. Over-Reliance on Equities: While stocks offer growth potential, relying too heavily on equities without adequate diversification can increase sequence of returns risk.

- **Tip:** Balance your portfolio with a mix of asset classes to manage risk.

Visual Aids

Example Chart: Impact of Sequence of Returns

Year	Market Return	Portfolio Value (Retiree A)	Portfolio Value (Retiree B)
0	-20%	$800,000	$1,200,000
1	-5%	$750,000	$1,140,000
2	10%	$800,000	$1,200,000
3	15%	$850,000	$1,320,000

Example Table: Dynamic Withdrawal Strategy

Year	Market Return	Portfolio Value	Withdrawal Percentage	Withdrawal Amount
1	+10%	$1,000,000	4%	$40,000
2	-10%	$900,000	3%	$27,000
3	+5%	$918,000	4%	$36,720
4	0%	$918,000	4%	$36,720

Example Chart: Buffer Asset Allocation

Asset Class	Allocation Amount	Time Horizon
Cash	$100,000	2-3 years of expenses
Bond/FIA	$200,000	3-5 years of expenses
Equities	$700,000	Long-term Growth

Conclusion of Chapter 3

Understanding sequence of returns risk is essential for effective retirement planning. By recognizing the potential impact of market volatility and implementing strategies such as diversification, dynamic withdrawals, maintaining buffer assets, and rebalancing, retirees can protect their portfolios and ensure a sustainable income throughout retirement. Mitigating sequence of returns risk helps preserve your savings and provides financial stability, even during periods of market uncertainty.

CHAPTER

FOUR

GROWTH PLANNING AND ASSET ALLOCATION

Importance of Growth in Retirement

Even in retirement, growth is essential to outpace inflation and ensure funds last throughout retirement. Proper asset allocation helps manage risk and optimize returns. A well-diversified portfolio can provide growth opportunities while minimizing the risk of significant losses.

Asset Allocation Strategies

Asset allocation involves spreading investments across different asset classes to balance risk and return. Here are the key strategies:

1. **Diversification:**
   - Spread investments across various asset classes (stocks, bonds, real estate) to reduce risk.
   - **Example:** A retiree might allocate 60% to equities, 30% to bonds, and 10% to real estate.

2. **Rebalancing:**

- Periodically adjust the portfolio to maintain the desired asset mix.

- **Example:** If market movements cause the equity portion of a portfolio to increase beyond the desired 60%, sell some equities and buy bonds or real estate to restore balance.

3. **Risk Tolerance Assessment:**
   - Align investments with the retiree's risk tolerance and time horizon.

   - **Example:** A conservative investor might favor bonds and cash, while a more aggressive investor might allocate more to equities.

Diversification and Risk Management

Diversification spreads risk across various investments, reducing the impact of any single asset's poor performance.

1. Geographical Diversification:
   - Invest in both domestic and international markets.

   - **Example:** A portfolio might include U.S. stocks, European stocks, and emerging market equities.

2. Sector Diversification:
   - Spread investments across different industries.

   - **Example:** Allocate funds to sectors like technology, healthcare, consumer goods, and energy.

3. Alternative Investments:

- Consider real estate, commodities, and other non-traditional assets for added diversification.

- **Example:** A portion of the portfolio might be invested in REITs (Real Estate Investment Trusts) or gold.

Case Studies and Examples

Case Study 1: Balanced Portfolio for Growth and Stability

John, a retiree with $1 million in savings, wants to balance growth and stability. He consults with his financial advisor and decides on the following allocation:

- **60% Equities:** $600,000 in a mix of U.S. and international stocks for growth potential.

- **30% Bonds/FIA's:** $300,000 in a mix of government and corporate bonds for income and stability.

- **10% Real Estate:** $100,000 in REITs for income and diversification.

Outcome:

- John's diversified portfolio provides growth opportunities while reducing the impact of market volatility.

- Regular rebalancing ensures the portfolio remains aligned with his risk tolerance and investment goals.

Case Study 2: Rebalancing During Market Volatility

Mary, a retiree with a $500,000 portfolio, experiences significant market volatility. Initially, her portfolio is allocated as follows:

- **50% Equities:** $250,000

- **40% Bonds/FIA's:** $200,000

- **10% Cash:** $50,000

During a market downturn, the value of her equities drops by 20%, reducing their value to $200,000. To maintain her desired asset allocation, Mary decides to rebalance:

- She sells $25,000 worth of bonds and invests it in equities, restoring the balance to 50% equities, 35% bonds, and 15% cash.

Outcome:
- By rebalancing, Mary takes advantage of lower equity prices and maintains her risk profile.

Case Study 3: Including Alternative Investments for Added Diversification

Tom and Lisa, a retired couple, want to enhance their portfolio's diversification. They decide to allocate a portion of their savings to alternative investments.

Strategy:
- Tom and Lisa allocate 10% of their portfolio to real estate and commodities.

- **10% Real Estate:** Invested in REITs.

- **5% Commodities:** Invested in gold and other commodities.

Outcome:

- The inclusion of alternative investments provides additional diversification, reducing the overall risk of their portfolio.

- They benefit from potential growth in the real estate and commodities markets.

Common Mistakes to Avoid

1. **Over-Allocation to Equities:** While stocks offer growth potential, too much exposure can increase risk, especially during market downturns.

   - **Example:** An overly aggressive portfolio might suffer significant losses during a market crash, impacting retirement security.

2. **Ignoring Inflation:** Underestimating the impact of inflation can erode purchasing power. Ensure a portion of the portfolio is allocated to growth assets.

   - **Tip:** Include assets like stocks and real estate that have historically outpaced inflation.

3. **Failing to Rebalance:** Not rebalancing can lead to unintended risk exposure. Regularly review and adjust the portfolio to maintain the desired allocation.

   - **Example:** Set a specific threshold (e.g., 5%) for when to rebalance your portfolio.

4. **Neglecting Diversification:** Concentrating investments in a single asset class or sector can increase risk. Diversify across various asset classes and sectors.

- **Tip:** Spread investments across different industries and geographical regions.

Visual Aids

Example Chart: Sample Asset Allocation

Asset Class	Allocation	Investment Type	Amount
Equities	60%	U.S. and International Stocks	$600,000
Bonds/FIA's	30%	Bonds or FIA's	$300,000
Real Estate	10%	Real Estate Investment Trusts	$100,000

Example Chart: Rebalancing During Market Volatility

Year	Equities	Bonds	Cash	Action
1	50%	40%	10%	Initial Allocation
2	40%	50%	10%	Market Drop
3	50%	35%	15%	Rebalance

Example Chart: Including Alternative Investments

Asset Class	Allocation	Investment Type	Amount
Equities	50%	U.S. and International Stocks	$600,000
Bonds/FIA's	30%	Bonds or FIA's	$300,000
Real Estate	10%	Real Estate Investment Trusts	$100,000
Commodities	10%	Gold and other commodities	$100,000

Conclusion of Chapter 4

Growth planning and asset allocation are critical components of a successful retirement strategy. By diversifying investments, regularly rebalancing the portfolio, and aligning asset allocation with risk tolerance and investment goals, retirees can achieve growth while managing risk. Proper growth planning ensures that retirement savings continue to grow, outpacing inflation and providing financial security throughout retirement.

CHAPTER

FIVE

TAX PLANNING FOR RETIREES

Overview of Tax Implications

Understanding the tax implications of retirement income is essential for maximizing after-tax income and preserving savings. Different types of retirement income are taxed differently, and effective tax planning can help minimize the tax burden.

Strategies for Tax Efficiency

1. **Tax Diversification:**

   - **Roth Accounts:** Contributions to Roth IRAs and Roth 401(k)s are made with after-tax dollars, and qualified withdrawals are tax-free.

   - **Traditional Accounts:** Contributions to traditional IRAs and 401(k)s are made with pre-tax dollars, and withdrawals are taxed as ordinary income.

   - **Taxable Accounts:** Investments in taxable brokerage accounts are subject to capital gains tax.

Example Strategy:

- Maintain a mix of traditional IRAs, Roth IRAs, and taxable accounts to provide flexibility in managing taxes.

- **Detailed Example:** John has $500,000 in a traditional IRA, $200,000 in a Roth IRA, and $300,000 in a taxable account. He plans his withdrawals to minimize his tax burden.

2. Strategic Withdrawals:

- **Sequence of Withdrawals:** The order in which you withdraw from different accounts can impact your tax liability.

- **Example:** Withdraw from taxable accounts first, followed by tax-deferred accounts, and finally Roth accounts to minimize taxes.

Detailed Example:

- John withdraws $20,000 from his taxable account first, using the capital gains tax rates.

- Once the taxable account is depleted, he withdraws $30,000 from his traditional IRA, paying ordinary income tax.

- Finally, he taps into his Roth IRA for tax-free withdrawals.

3. Roth Conversions:

- Converting funds from a traditional IRA to a Roth IRA can provide tax-free withdrawals in the future.

- **Timing:** Consider converting during years with lower income to reduce the tax impact.

Detailed Example:

- Susan, age 60, converts $50,000 from her traditional IRA to a Roth IRA each year for five years.

- She pays taxes on the converted amount at her current lower tax rate, resulting in tax-free withdrawals during retirement.

4. **Required Minimum Distributions (RMDs):**

- RMDs are mandatory withdrawals from traditional IRAs and 401(k)s starting at age 72.

- **Strategy:** Plan for RMDs in advance to manage taxable income and avoid penalties.

Detailed Example:

- Tom, age 72, has $1 million in his traditional IRA. His RMD for the year is approximately $39,062.50.

- By planning for RMDs, Tom manages his taxable income and ensures he withdraws the required amount.

5. **Tax-Efficient Investments:**

- **Municipal Bonds:** Interest from municipal bonds is typically tax-free at the federal level and possibly at the state level.

- **Index Funds:** These funds tend to have lower turnover and generate fewer taxable events.

Detailed Example:

- Mary allocates a portion of her portfolio to municipal bonds, providing tax-free interest income.

- She also invests in index funds for tax-efficient growth with minimal capital gains.

Case Studies and Examples

Case Study 1: Tax Diversification for Retirement Income

John and Mary, both 65, have saved $1 million for retirement, divided among different accounts:

- **$400,000 in a Traditional IRA**

- **$300,000 in a Roth IRA**

- **$300,000 in a Taxable Brokerage Account**

Strategy:

- John and Mary plan to withdraw from their taxable account first, using the capital gains tax rates.

- Once their taxable account is depleted, they will withdraw from their traditional IRA, paying ordinary income tax.

- Finally, they will tap into their Roth IRA for tax-free withdrawals.

Outcome:

- This strategy allows John and Mary to manage their tax liability and potentially stay in a lower tax bracket.

Case Study 2: Roth Conversion to Manage Future Taxes

Susan, age 60, is planning her retirement strategy. She has $500,000 in a traditional IRA and expects her tax rate to be higher in the future.

Strategy:

- Susan decides to convert $100,000 from her traditional IRA to a Roth IRA each year for five years.

- She pays taxes on the converted amount at her current lower tax rate.

Outcome:

- By the time Susan retires, she has a significant amount in her Roth IRA, providing tax-free income in retirement.

Case Study 3: Managing RMDs to Avoid Penalties

Tom, age 72, has $1 million in his traditional IRA. He is required to take RMDs to avoid penalties.

Strategy:

- Tom calculates his RMDs and plans withdrawals to manage his taxable income.

- He also considers making qualified charitable distributions (QCDs) to satisfy his RMD requirements while supporting his favorite charities.

Outcome:

- Tom successfully manages his RMDs, avoids penalties, and supports charitable causes.

Common Mistakes to Avoid

1. **Ignoring RMDs:** Failing to take RMDs can result in hefty penalties. Plan for these withdrawals to manage taxable income effectively.

   - **Tip:** Work with a financial advisor to calculate and plan for RMDs.

2. **Overlooking Roth Conversions:** Missing out on the opportunity to convert traditional IRA funds to a Roth IRA can lead to higher taxes in the future.

   - **Tip:** Consider Roth conversions during lower-income years.

3. **Not Considering State Taxes:** State tax implications can vary, so consider both federal and state taxes in your planning.

   - **Example:** Some states tax Social Security benefits, while others do not.

4. **Underestimating Healthcare Costs:** Healthcare expenses can be significant in retirement and may provide opportunities for tax deductions.

   - **Tip:** Keep track of medical expenses to take advantage of potential deductions.

Visual Aids

Example Chart: Sequence of Withdrawals

Year	Source of Withdrawal	Amount	Tax Implication
1-5	Taxable Brokerage Account	$50,000	Capital Gains Tax

| 6-10 | Traditional IRA | $50,000 | Ordinary Income Tax |
| 11+ | Roth IRA | $50,000 | Tax-Free Withdrawals |

Example Chart: Roth Conversion Strategy

Year	Amount Converted	Tax Rate	Taxes Paid	Roth IRA Value
1	$50,000	12%	$6,000	$50,000
2	$50,000	12%	$6,000	$102,000
3	$50,000	12%	$6,000	$157,080
4	$50,000	12%	$6,000	$215,942
5	$50,000	12%	$6,000	$278,858

Example Table: RMD Calculation

Age	Account Balance	RMD Factor	RMD Amount
72	$1,000,000	25.6	$39,062.50
73	$980,000	24.7	$39,676.11
74	$960,000	23.8	$40,336.13

Conclusion of Chapter 5

Effective tax planning is essential for maximizing retirement income and preserving savings. By understanding the tax implications of different income sources and implementing strategies such as tax diversification, strategic withdrawals, Roth conversions, and tax-efficient investments, retirees can minimize their tax burden and enhance their financial security. Proper tax planning ensures that more of your hard-earned savings stay with you, providing a more comfortable and worry-free retirement.

CHAPTER

SIX

HEALTHCARE AND LONG-TERM CARE PLANNING

Importance of Healthcare Planning

Healthcare costs can be one of the most significant expenses in retirement. Proper planning for healthcare and long-term care ensures that you have the necessary resources to cover these costs without depleting your savings.

Medicare and Supplemental Insurance

Medicare is the federal health insurance program for people aged 65 and older, as well as some younger individuals with disabilities. Understanding Medicare and supplementing it with additional insurance can help manage healthcare expenses.

1. **Medicare Parts:**

   - **Part A (Hospital Insurance):** Covers inpatient hospital stays, skilled nursing facility care, hospice care, and some home health care.

- **Part B (Medical Insurance):** Covers certain doctors' services, outpatient care, medical supplies, and preventive services.

- **Part D (Prescription Drug Coverage):** Helps cover the cost of prescription drugs.

- **Medicare Advantage (Part C):** An alternative to Original Medicare that offers additional benefits through private insurance companies.

2. **Supplemental Insurance:**

- **Medigap:** Private health insurance that helps pay some of the healthcare costs that Original Medicare doesn't cover, such as copayments, coinsurance, and deductibles.

- **Medicare Advantage Plans:** These plans often include additional benefits like dental, vision, and wellness programs.

3. **Enrollment Periods:**

- **Initial Enrollment Period:** Begins three months before you turn 65 and ends three months after the month you turn 65.

- **General Enrollment Period:** January 1 to March 31 each year, for those who missed their initial enrollment.

- **Special Enrollment Periods:** For specific circumstances, such as losing employer coverage.

Detailed Examples:

- **John:** Enrolls in Medicare Part A and Part B at age 65 and purchases a Medigap policy to cover additional expenses.

- **Mary:** Chooses a Medicare Advantage Plan that includes dental and vision coverage.

Long-Term Care Options and Strategies

Long-term care (LTC) involves a variety of services to meet health or personal care needs over an extended period. Planning for LTC is essential to protect your retirement savings.

1. **Types of Long-Term Care:**

   - **Home Care:** Assistance with daily activities provided in the individual's home.

   - **Assisted Living:** Housing, meals, and personal care services for those who need help with daily activities but do not require full-time nursing care.

   - **Nursing Homes:** Provide a higher level of medical care and personal care services.

2. **Paying for Long-Term Care:**

   - **Personal Savings:** Using personal assets to pay for care.

   - **Long-Term Care Insurance:** Insurance specifically designed to cover long-term care expenses.

   - **Medicaid:** A state and federal program that helps with medical costs for some people with limited income and resources. Medicaid also offers benefits not normally covered by Medicare, like nursing home care and personal care services.

- **Hybrid Policies:** Life insurance or annuities with long-term care riders.

3. **Long-Term Care Insurance:**
   - **Benefits:** Covers a range of services, including home care, assisted living, and nursing home care.
   - **Cost:** Premiums are based on age, health, and the level of coverage.
   - **Considerations:** When purchasing, consider the elimination period, benefit period, and inflation protection.

Detailed Examples:
   - **Tom and Lisa:** Purchase a long-term care insurance policy with a daily benefit of $200, a benefit period of 3 years, and an inflation protection rider.
   - **Susan:** Decides to use a hybrid life insurance policy with a long-term care rider, providing both a death benefit and coverage for long-term care expenses.

Case Studies and Examples

Case Study 1: Medicare and Supplemental Insurance Planning

John is turning 65 and is planning his healthcare coverage. He decides to enroll in Original Medicare (Part A and Part B) and purchases a Medigap policy to cover additional expenses.

Scenario:

- John uses Medicare Part A and Part B for his primary healthcare needs.

- His Medigap policy covers copayments, coinsurance, and deductibles, reducing his out-of-pocket expenses.

- John also enrolls in a Medicare Part D plan to cover his prescription medications.

Outcome:

- John has comprehensive healthcare coverage with minimal out-of-pocket costs.

Case Study 2: Long-Term Care Insurance

Mary, age 60, is concerned about potential long-term care costs in the future. She decides to purchase a long-term care insurance policy.

Strategy:

- Mary chooses a policy with a benefit of $200 per day for a benefit period of 3 years.

- Her policy includes an inflation protection rider to ensure her benefits keep pace with rising costs.

Outcome:

- If Mary needs long-term care, her insurance will cover a significant portion of the costs, protecting her retirement savings.

- The inflation protection rider ensures that her benefits will be adequate even if she requires care many years into the future.

Case Study 3: Using Hybrid Policies for Long-Term Care

Tom and Lisa, both 65, want to ensure they are covered for long-term care without losing the value of their premiums if they do not need care. They decide to use hybrid life insurance policies with long-term care riders.

Strategy:

- Tom and Lisa each purchase a life insurance policy with a long-term care rider.

- The policies provide a death benefit if they do not need long-term care and coverage for long-term care expenses if they do.

Outcome:

- Tom and Lisa have the peace of mind knowing that they are covered for long-term care expenses.

- If they do not need long-term care, their heirs will receive the death benefit from the life insurance policies.

Common Mistakes to Avoid

1. **Delaying Enrollment in Medicare:** Missing the initial enrollment period can result in higher premiums and late enrollment penalties.

- o **Tip:** Enroll in Medicare during the initial enrollment period to avoid penalties.

2. Not Considering Medigap or Medicare Advantage: Relying solely on Original Medicare can lead to high out-of-pocket costs. Supplemental insurance can provide additional coverage and reduce expenses.

   - o **Example:** Medigap policies can cover copayments, coinsurance, and deductibles not covered by Medicare.

3. **Underestimating Long-Term Care Costs:** Long-term care can be expensive, and failing to plan for it can deplete retirement savings.

   - o **Tip:** Consider purchasing long-term care insurance or using hybrid policies to cover potential expenses.

4. **Ignoring Long-Term Care Insurance:** While premiums can be high, long-term care insurance can provide significant financial protection. Consider purchasing a policy while still in good health to secure lower premiums.

   - o **Example:** Premiums are generally lower when purchased at a younger age and in good health.

Visual Aids

Example Chart: Medicare and Supplemental Insurance Overview

Coverage Type	Services Covered	Enrollment Periods
Medicare Part A	Inpatient hospital stays, skilled nursing, hospice	Initial, General, Special

Medicare Part B	Doctor services, outpatient care, preventive services	Initial, General, Special
Medicare Part D	Prescription drugs	Initial, General, Special
Medigap	Copayments, coinsurance, deductibles	Initial, General, Special
Medicare Advantage	All Part A and B services, may include additional benefits	Initial, General, Special

Example Chart: Long-Term Care Insurance Benefits

Policy Feature	Description
Daily Benefit Amount	The amount the policy will pay per day for care
Benefit Period	The length of time the benefits will be paid
Elimination Period	The waiting period before benefits begin
Inflation Protection	Adjusts benefits to keep pace with inflation

Example Table: Hybrid Policies vs. Traditional Long-Term Care Insurance

Feature	Hybrid Policy	Traditional LTC Insurance
Death Benefit	Yes	No
Long-Term Care Coverage	Yes	Yes
Premiums	Higher, but part goes to life insurance	Lower, but used solely for LTC
Flexibility	Provides coverage for LTC and a death benefit	Provides coverage solely for LTC

Conclusion of Chapter 6

Healthcare and long-term care planning are critical components of a comprehensive retirement strategy. By understanding Medicare, supplementing it with additional insurance, and planning for potential long-term care needs, retirees can manage healthcare expenses and protect their savings. Proper planning ensures that you have the resources to cover medical and personal care costs, providing peace of mind and financial security throughout retirement.

CHAPTER

SEVEN

ESTATE PLANNING ESSENTIALS

Importance of Estate Planning

Estate planning ensures that your assets are distributed according to your wishes after your death. It also helps minimize taxes, legal fees, and other expenses, and provides clear instructions for managing your affairs if you become incapacitated.

Key Documents and Considerations

1. **Will:**

   - A legal document that specifies how your assets should be distributed after your death.

   - Names an executor to manage your estate and guardians for minor children.

   - **Detailed Example:** John and Mary create a will that outlines the distribution of their assets, names a guardian for their minor children, and appoints an executor to handle their estate.

2. **Trust:**

- A legal arrangement where a trustee holds and manages assets for the benefit of beneficiaries.

- Can be used to avoid probate, reduce estate taxes, and provide for minor children or special needs beneficiaries.

- **Types of Trusts:**

  - **Revocable Living Trust:** Can be changed or revoked by the grantor. Helps avoid probate.

  - **Irrevocable Trust:** Cannot be changed once established. Can help reduce estate taxes and protect assets from creditors.

  - **Special Needs Trust:** Provides for a disabled beneficiary without affecting their eligibility for government benefits.

- **Detailed Example:** Susan sets up a revocable living trust to manage her assets, avoid probate, and ensure a smooth transition of her estate to her heirs.

3. **Durable Power of Attorney:**

- A document that grants someone the authority to manage your financial affairs if you become incapacitated.

- **Detailed Example:** Tom appoints his daughter as his durable power of attorney to manage his finances if he becomes unable to do so.

4. **Healthcare Proxy and Living Will:**

- A healthcare proxy designates someone to make medical decisions on your behalf.

- A living will outline your wishes for medical treatment in case you are unable to communicate them.

- **Detailed Example:** Lisa creates a healthcare proxy and living will to ensure her healthcare decisions are made according to her wishes.

5. **Beneficiary Designations:**

   - Ensure that beneficiary designations on retirement accounts, life insurance policies, and other assets are up-to-date.

   - **Detailed Example:** John updates the beneficiary designations on his retirement accounts and life insurance policies to reflect his current wishes.

6. **Letter of Intent:**

   - A document that provides guidance to your executor and beneficiaries about your wishes and instructions.

   - **Detailed Example:** Mary writes a letter of intent to her executor outlining her wishes for her funeral arrangements and the distribution of personal belongings.

Planning for a Surviving Spouse

Ensuring that your surviving spouse is financially secure is a critical aspect of estate planning. Consider the following strategies:

1. **Joint Ownership:**
   - Holding assets jointly with rights of survivorship ensures that the surviving spouse automatically inherits the assets without going through probate.

   - **Detailed Example:** John and Mary hold their home and bank accounts jointly, ensuring that these assets pass directly to the surviving spouse.

2. **Life Insurance:**
   - Provides financial support to your spouse in the event of your death. Consider term life or permanent life insurance policies based on your needs.

   - **Detailed Example:** Tom purchases a term life insurance policy to provide financial support for his spouse in case of his untimely death.

3. **Retirement Accounts:**
   - Designate your spouse as the primary beneficiary on retirement accounts to allow for spousal rollovers, which preserve tax benefits.

   - **Detailed Example:** Susan designates her husband as the primary beneficiary on her 401(k) and IRA accounts.

4. **Trusts:**
   - Setting up a marital trust (also known as an "A-B Trust" or "QTIP Trust") can provide income to your spouse while preserving the principal for other beneficiaries.

- **Detailed Example:** John and Mary establish a marital trust to provide income for the surviving spouse while preserving the estate for their children.

Case Studies and Examples

Case Study 1: Establishing a Trust for Minor Children

John and Mary have two young children and want to ensure their financial security if something happens to them. They decide to set up a revocable living trust.

Scenario:

- John and Mary transfer their major assets, including their home and investment accounts, into the trust.

- They appoint a trustee to manage the trust assets for their children until they reach adulthood.

- The trust outlines how the assets should be used for their children's education, healthcare, and living expenses.

Outcome:

- John and Mary ensure that their children are financially secure and that the assets are managed according to their wishes.

Case Study 2: Using Life Insurance for Estate Planning

Susan, a widow with two adult children, wants to ensure that her estate is distributed according to her wishes and that her children are financially secure.

Strategy:

- Susan purchases a $500,000 life insurance policy with her children as beneficiaries.

- She sets up a revocable living trust to manage her assets and distribute them according to her instructions.

- The life insurance proceeds provide immediate financial support to her children, while the trust assets are managed and distributed over time.

Outcome:

- Susan's children receive immediate financial support from the life insurance policy and benefit from the managed distribution of trust assets.

Case Study 3: Planning for a Surviving Spouse

Tom and Lisa want to ensure that the surviving spouse is financially secure. They decide to use a combination of joint ownership, life insurance, and trusts.

Strategy:

- Tom and Lisa hold their major assets jointly with rights of survivorship.

- They each purchase life insurance policies to provide financial support for the surviving spouse.

- They establish a marital trust to provide income for the surviving spouse while preserving the principal for their children.

Outcome:

- The surviving spouse inherits the jointly held assets without going through probate.

- The life insurance policies provide immediate financial support.

- The marital trust ensures a steady income stream for the surviving spouse while preserving the estate for their children.

Common Mistakes to Avoid

1. **Not Having a Will:** Dying without a will (intestate) can lead to state laws determining how your assets are distributed, which may not align with your wishes.

   - **Tip:** Create a will to ensure your assets are distributed according to your wishes.

2. **Failing to Update Documents:** Regularly update your will, trust, and beneficiary designations to reflect changes in your family situation and financial circumstances.

   - **Example:** Update your estate planning documents after significant life events, such as marriage, divorce, the birth of a child, or the death of a spouse.

3. **Ignoring Estate Taxes:** Large estates may be subject to federal and state estate taxes. Planning strategies, such as gifting and trusts, can help minimize these taxes.

   - **Tip:** Work with an estate planning attorney to develop strategies to minimize estate taxes.

4. **Not Communicating Your Plan:** Ensure that your executor, trustee, and beneficiaries understand your estate plan and their roles.

- **Tip:** Discuss your estate plan with your family and key individuals to ensure everyone is aware of your wishes and their responsibilities.

Visual Aids

Example Chart: Key Estate Planning Documents

Document	Purpose	Who Needs It
Will	Distribute assets, name executor, appoint guardians	Everyone
Trust	Manage assets, avoid probate, reduce taxes	Those with significant assets
Durable Power of Attorney	Manage financial affairs if incapacitated	Everyone
Healthcare Proxy & Living Will	Make medical decisions, outline treatment wishes	Everyone
Beneficiary Designations	Ensure assets go to the intended beneficiaries	Everyone
Letter of Intent	Provide guidance to executor and beneficiaries	Everyone

Example Chart: Trust vs. Will

Feature	Trust	Will
Probate	Avoids probate	Goes through probate
Privacy	Keeps estate details private	Becomes public record
Control	Provides detailed control over assets	Limited control after distribution

Flexibility	Can be amended or revoked	Can be amended with a codicil or new will

Example Table: Planning for a Surviving Spouse

Strategy	Description
Joint Ownership	Automatically transfers assets to the surviving spouse
Life Insurance	Provides financial support to the surviving spouse
Retirement Accounts	Designate spouse as primary beneficiary for spousal rollovers
Marital Trust	Provides income to the surviving spouse while preserving principal for other beneficiaries

Conclusion of Chapter 7

Estate planning is an essential part of a comprehensive retirement strategy. By creating key documents such as a will, trust, durable power of attorney, and healthcare proxy, and by ensuring that beneficiary designations are up-to-date, you can ensure that your assets are distributed according to your wishes and that your loved ones are provided for. Proper estate planning minimizes legal fees, taxes, and other expenses, providing peace of mind and financial security for you and your family.

EIGHT

NON-FINANCIAL ASPECTS OF RETIREMENT

Finding Purpose and Fulfillment

Retirement is not just about financial security; it's also about finding purpose and fulfillment. As you transition into this new phase of life, it's essential to focus on activities and relationships that bring joy and meaning.

1. **Reflect on Your Passions:**
   - Identify activities and interests that you are passionate about.
   - Consider how you can incorporate these into your daily routine.
   - **Detailed Example:** John, a retired engineer, discovers a passion for woodworking. He sets up a workshop in his garage and spends his days creating furniture and crafts.

2. **Set New Goals:**

- Establish new personal and professional goals to maintain a sense of purpose.

- Goals could include learning a new skill, volunteering, or starting a part-time business.

- **Detailed Example:** Mary sets a goal to learn Spanish. She enrolls in a local language class and plans a trip to Spain to immerse herself in the language and culture.

3. **Pursue Lifelong Learning:**

- Engage in lifelong learning opportunities, such as taking courses, attending workshops, or joining clubs.

- Explore topics that interest you, whether they are related to hobbies, personal growth, or professional development.

- **Detailed Example:** Tom enrolls in a series of online courses on digital photography. He joins a local photography club and starts participating in photo contests and exhibitions.

Relationship Building and Social Connections

Maintaining and building social connections is crucial for emotional well-being and can greatly enhance your retirement experience.

1. **Strengthen Existing Relationships:**

- Invest time in nurturing relationships with family and friends.

- Plan regular activities and gatherings to stay connected.

- **Detailed Example:** Susan organizes a weekly family dinner where her children and grandchildren come together to share a meal and bond.

2. **Expand Your Social Circle:**
   - Join clubs, groups, or organizations that align with your interests.
   - Participate in community events or volunteer opportunities to meet new people.
   - **Detailed Example:** John joins a local hiking club, where he meets like-minded individuals and explores new trails every weekend.

3. **Stay Connected Digitally:**
   - Use technology to stay in touch with loved ones who live far away.
   - Join online communities or social media groups related to your interests.
   - **Detailed Example:** Mary uses video calls to stay connected with her grandchildren who live in another state. She also joins an online book club where she discusses literature with people from around the world.

Hobbies, Travel, and Personal Growth

Retirement is an excellent time to explore hobbies, travel, and focus on personal growth. These activities can provide a sense of accomplishment and enjoyment.

I. **Explore Hobbies:**
   - Revisit old hobbies or discover new ones.
   - Consider hobbies that are both enjoyable and mentally stimulating, such as gardening, painting, or playing a musical instrument.
   - **Detailed Example:** Tom takes up gardening, turning his backyard into a beautiful oasis of flowers and vegetables. He finds joy in nurturing plants and spending time outdoors.

II. **Travel:**
   - Plan trips to destinations you've always wanted to visit.
   - Travel can provide new experiences and a sense of adventure.
   - Consider group travel or travel clubs for social interaction and shared experiences.
   - **Detailed Example:** Susan joins a travel club and goes on a guided tour of Europe. She visits historic landmarks, tries new cuisines, and makes lasting friendships with fellow travelers.

III. **Personal Growth:**
   - Focus on personal development through meditation, mindfulness, or spiritual practices.
   - Set aside time for physical fitness, such as yoga, walking, or strength training.

- **Detailed Example:** Mary starts a daily yoga and meditation practice, which helps her stay physically fit and mentally centered. She also attends a weekly mindfulness group.

Case Studies and Examples

Case Study 1: Finding New Purpose Through Volunteering

John, a recent retiree, felt a void after leaving his long-time career. He decided to explore volunteering opportunities in his community.

Scenario:

- John started volunteering at a local animal shelter and found great fulfillment in helping animals and connecting with other volunteers.

- He also began mentoring young professionals in his former industry, which allowed him to share his expertise and stay engaged.

Outcome:

- John experiences a renewed sense of purpose and fulfillment, knowing that he is making a positive impact in his community.

Case Study 2: Building Social Connections Through Hobbies

Mary, a widow in her 70s, was looking for ways to stay active and meet new people. She decided to join a local gardening club and a book club.

Scenario:

- Mary made new friends who shared her interests and looked forward to the regular meetings and activities.

- The social interactions and shared passions significantly improved her emotional well-being and sense of belonging.

Outcome:

- Mary finds joy and companionship through her hobbies, enhancing her overall quality of life.

Case Study 3: Pursuing Lifelong Learning

Susan, a former teacher, retired at 65 but still had a passion for learning and teaching. She decided to take up online courses and participate in community education programs.

Scenario:

- Susan enrolled in several online courses on subjects she was curious about, such as art history and digital photography.

- She also began teaching adult education classes at the local community center, which kept her engaged and fulfilled.

Outcome:

- Susan stays mentally active and enjoys the satisfaction of learning new things and sharing her knowledge with others.

Common Mistakes to Avoid

1. Losing Sense of Purpose: Retirement can sometimes lead to a loss of identity and purpose. Actively seek activities that provide meaning and fulfillment.

- **Tip:** Set new goals and pursue activities that you are passionate about.

2. Neglecting Social Connections: Isolation can negatively impact mental and emotional health. Prioritize building and maintaining relationships.

- **Example:** Join clubs, groups, or volunteer organizations to meet new people and stay connected.

3.Ignoring Physical and Mental Health: Staying active and engaged is crucial for overall well-being. Incorporate regular physical exercise and mental stimulation into your routine.

- **Tip:** Explore activities such as yoga, walking, and lifelong learning to stay physically and mentally fit.

4. Overlooking Personal Growth: Retirement is a time for personal development. Embrace opportunities for learning and self-improvement.

- **Tip:** Consider practices such as meditation, mindfulness, and spiritual growth to enhance your personal development.

Visual Aids

Example Chart: Non-Financial Retirement Planning

Aspect	Activities	Benefits
Finding Purpose	Volunteering, setting new goals, lifelong learning	Sense of fulfillment, continued growth
Social Connections	Strengthening existing relationships, expanding social circle, staying connected digitally	Improved emotional well-being, reduced isolation
Hobbies and Travel	Exploring hobbies, planning travel, joining clubs	Enjoyment, adventure, new experiences
Personal Growth	Meditation, fitness, personal development	Better mental and physical health

Example Chart: Benefits of Lifelong Learning

Activity	Benefits
Taking Courses	Mental stimulation, skill development
Attending Workshops	Hands-on learning, networking opportunities
Joining Clubs	Social interaction, shared interests
Teaching Others	Sharing knowledge, staying engaged

Example Table: Physical and Mental Health Activities

Activity	Description	Benefits
Yoga	Physical exercises combined with breathing and meditation	Improved flexibility, reduced stress
Walking	Regular walks in nature or around the neighborhood	Cardiovascular health, mental clarity

Meditation	Mindfulness and relaxation techniques	Reduced anxiety, better focus
Lifelong Learning	Taking courses, reading, attending lectures	Mental stimulation, continued personal growth

Conclusion of Chapter 8

Retirement is a significant life transition that offers an opportunity to redefine your purpose and find new sources of fulfillment. By focusing on building relationships, pursuing hobbies and travel, and engaging in lifelong learning and personal growth, you can create a rich, rewarding retirement experience. Embracing the non-financial aspects of retirement ensures a balanced and satisfying life, enhancing your overall well-being.

CHAPTER

NINE

INTEGRATING ALL COMPONENTS INTO A COHESIVE PLAN

Importance of a Holistic Approach

Creating a successful retirement strategy requires integrating all components—financial, healthcare, estate planning, and personal fulfillment—into a cohesive plan. A holistic approach ensures that every aspect of your retirement is considered and addressed, providing comprehensive security and peace of mind.

How to Integrate Income, Growth, Tax, Healthcare, and Estate Planning

1. **Income and Growth Planning:**

   - **Income Sources:** Identify and coordinate all income sources, including Social Security, pensions, annuities, and investment withdrawals.

   - **Growth Planning:** Ensure your portfolio is balanced between growth and preservation to outpace inflation and sustain your lifestyle.

- **Withdrawal Strategies:** Implement dynamic withdrawal strategies that adapt to market conditions and personal needs.

Detailed Example:

- **Scenario:** John has $1 million in retirement savings divided among a traditional IRA, a Roth IRA, and a taxable brokerage account. He also receives Social Security and a small pension.

- **Integration:** John works with his financial advisor to create a withdrawal strategy that minimizes taxes and maximizes his income. He withdraws from his taxable account first, followed by his traditional IRA, and lastly from his Roth IRA.

2. **Tax Planning:**

- **Tax-Efficient Withdrawals:** Plan withdrawals in a tax-efficient manner to minimize tax liability.

- **Roth Conversions:** Consider converting traditional IRA funds to a Roth IRA during lower-income years.

- **Tax Diversification:** Maintain a mix of taxable, tax-deferred, and tax-free accounts to provide flexibility in managing taxes.

Detailed Example:

- **Scenario:** Susan, age 65, has $500,000 in a traditional IRA, $200,000 in a Roth IRA, and $300,000 in a taxable account.

- **Integration:** She plans to convert $50,000 from her traditional IRA to her Roth IRA each year for five years, paying taxes at her current lower rate and ensuring tax-free withdrawals in the future.

3. **Healthcare and Long-Term Care Planning:**

   - **Medicare and Supplemental Insurance:** Ensure you have adequate healthcare coverage through Medicare and supplemental insurance.

   - **Long-Term Care Insurance:** Evaluate the need for long-term care insurance to protect your assets and provide for future care needs.

   - **Healthcare Directives:** Establish healthcare proxies and living wills to communicate your healthcare wishes.

   Detailed Example:

   - **Scenario:** Tom, age 70, has Medicare Parts A and B, a Medigap policy, and a long-term care insurance policy.

   - **Integration:** Tom reviews his healthcare coverage annually with his advisor to ensure it meets his needs. He also updates his healthcare directives to reflect his current wishes.

4. **Estate Planning:**

   - **Wills and Trusts:** Create or update your will and consider establishing trusts to manage and distribute your assets.

   - **Beneficiary Designations:** Review and update beneficiary designations on all accounts and policies.

- **Power of Attorney:** Designate a durable power of attorney for financial and healthcare decisions.

Detailed Example:

- **Scenario:** Lisa, age 72, has a revocable living trust, a will, and updated beneficiary designations on all her accounts.

- **Integration:** She reviews her estate plan every few years or after major life events to ensure it aligns with her wishes.

5. **Personal Fulfillment:**

- **Goals and Passions:** Set personal goals and pursue activities that bring joy and fulfillment.

- **Social Connections:** Build and maintain relationships through social activities and community involvement.

- **Lifelong Learning and Hobbies:** Engage in lifelong learning and hobbies to stay mentally and physically active.

Detailed Example:

- **Scenario:** Mary, a recent retiree, sets a goal to travel to all seven continents. She joins a travel club and plans trips with friends and family.

- **Integration:** Mary also takes up painting, enrolling in local art classes and participating in community art shows.

Case Studies and Examples

Case Study 1: Comprehensive Retirement Plan

John and Mary, both 65, are preparing for retirement. They work with a financial advisor to create a comprehensive plan that integrates all aspects of their retirement.

Scenario:

- **Income Planning:** They plan to draw from their taxable accounts first, followed by traditional IRAs, and lastly, their Roth IRAs to minimize taxes.

- **Growth and Risk Management:** Their portfolio is balanced with 60% equities and 40% bonds to provide growth while managing risk.

- **Healthcare and Long-Term Care:** They have Medicare Parts A and B, a Medigap policy, and long-term care insurance.

- **Estate Planning:** They establish a revocable living trust and update their wills and beneficiary designations.

- **Personal Fulfillment:** They set goals to travel, volunteer, and pursue hobbies like gardening and photography.

Outcome:

- John and Mary have a clear, integrated plan that covers their financial, healthcare, and personal needs, providing peace of mind and security.

Case Study 2: Adjusting the Plan Over Time

Susan, 70, regularly reviews her retirement plan with her advisor to ensure it remains aligned with her goals and needs.

Scenario:

- **Income Adjustments:** Susan adjusts her withdrawal strategy based on market performance, reducing withdrawals during downturns.

- **Tax Planning:** She converts a portion of her traditional IRA to a Roth IRA during a year with lower taxable income.

- **Healthcare Updates:** Susan reviews and updates her healthcare directives and ensures her insurance coverage is adequate.

- **Personal Fulfillment:** She joins a travel club and takes up painting to stay engaged and fulfilled.

Outcome:

- Susan's proactive approach and regular reviews ensure her plan remains relevant and effective, adapting to changes in her life and the market.

Case Study 3: Balancing Growth and Stability

Tom and Lisa, both 67, want to ensure their retirement savings continue to grow while maintaining stability.

Scenario:

- **Income Sources:** They receive Social Security, a pension, and draw from their investment accounts.

- **Portfolio Allocation:** Their portfolio is allocated 50% to equities, 30% to bonds, 10% to real estate, and 10% to cash.

- **Tax Planning:** They use tax-efficient withdrawal strategies to manage their tax liability.

- **Healthcare and Estate Planning:** They have comprehensive healthcare coverage and updated estate planning documents.

- **Personal Fulfillment:** They volunteer at a local animal shelter and pursue hobbies like hiking and photography.

Outcome:

- Tom and Lisa's integrated plan provides financial stability, growth, and personal fulfillment, ensuring a balanced and satisfying retirement.

Common Mistakes to Avoid

1. **Lack of Coordination:** Failing to integrate different aspects of your retirement plan can lead to gaps in coverage and inefficiencies.

   - **Tip:** Work with a financial advisor to create a cohesive plan that addresses all aspects of retirement.

2. **Infrequent Reviews:** Not regularly reviewing and adjusting your plan can result in outdated strategies that no longer align with your goals or circumstances.

   - **Example:** Schedule annual reviews with your advisor to ensure your plan remains relevant.

3. **Neglecting Personal Fulfillment:** Focusing solely on financial planning without considering personal fulfillment can lead to a lackluster retirement experience.

   - **Tip:** Set personal goals and pursue activities that bring joy and meaning to your life.

4. **Overlooking Tax Implications:** Ignoring the tax impact of withdrawals and income can result in higher taxes and reduced income.

   - **Tip:** Implement tax-efficient strategies and consult with a tax professional.

Visual Aids

Example Chart: Integrated Retirement Plan Components

Component	Key Elements	Action Steps
Income and Growth Planning	Social Security, pensions, investments	Identify sources, balance growth and preservation
Tax Planning	Tax-efficient withdrawals, Roth conversions	Plan withdrawals, consider Roth conversions
Healthcare Planning	Medicare, Medigap, long-term care insurance	Ensure coverage, establish directives
Estate Planning	Wills, trusts, beneficiary designations	Create/update documents, review designations
Personal Fulfillment	Goals, hobbies, social connections	Set goals, engage in activities, build relationships

Example Chart: Annual Review Checklist

Review Area	Key Actions
Financial Goals	Reassess goals, adjust plans if needed
Investment Performance	Review portfolio, rebalance if necessary
Income Needs	Adjust withdrawal strategy, update budget
Estate Planning	Update wills, trusts, and beneficiary designations
Healthcare and Long-Term Care	Review coverage, update directives
Policy Changes	Stay informed, adjust plan based on new laws

Conclusion of Chapter 9

Integrating all components into a cohesive retirement plan is essential for a secure and fulfilling retirement. By coordinating income, growth, tax, healthcare, and estate planning with personal fulfillment goals, retirees can ensure a comprehensive approach that addresses all aspects of their lives. Regular reviews and adjustments help keep the plan relevant and effective, providing peace of mind and a clear path to achieving retirement goals.

TEN

REVIEWING AND ADJUSTING YOUR PLAN

Importance of Regular Reviews

Regularly reviewing and adjusting your retirement plan is crucial for ensuring that it remains aligned with your goals, needs, and any changes in your financial situation or the market. Life events, market conditions, and policy changes can all impact your retirement strategy, making periodic reviews essential.

How to Adjust Your Plan Over Time

1. **Annual Reviews:**

   - Conduct a comprehensive review of your retirement plan at least once a year.

   - Assess your financial goals, investment performance, income needs, and any changes in your personal circumstances.

Detailed Example:

- **Scenario:** John, age 65, conducts an annual review of his retirement plan with his financial advisor.

- **Integration:** They reassess his goals, review his investment performance, adjust his withdrawal strategy, and update his estate planning documents.

2. **Life Events:**

- Adjust your plan in response to significant life events such as marriage, divorce, the birth of a child, or the death of a spouse.

- Revisit your estate planning documents and beneficiary designations to ensure they reflect your current wishes.

Detailed Example:

- **Scenario:** Mary, age 70, experiences the birth of her first grandchild. She updates her will and beneficiary designations to include her new grandchild.

- **Integration:** She also adjusts her financial plan to include a fund for her grandchild's education.

3. **Market Conditions:**

- Evaluate the impact of market conditions on your portfolio and adjust your investment strategy as needed.

- Consider rebalancing your portfolio to maintain the desired asset allocation and risk profile.

Detailed Example:

- **Scenario:** Tom, age 68, experiences a significant market downturn. His portfolio is heavily weighted in equities, which have lost value.

- **Integration:** Tom and his advisor decide to rebalance his portfolio by shifting some assets from equities to bonds to reduce risk.

4. Policy Changes:

- Stay informed about changes in tax laws, Social Security policies, and healthcare regulations that may affect your retirement plan.

- Adjust your plan to take advantage of new opportunities or mitigate the impact of unfavorable changes.

Detailed Example:

- **Scenario:** Susan, age 72, learns of changes in tax laws that affect her required minimum distributions (RMDs).

- **Integration:** She adjusts her withdrawal strategy to optimize her tax situation and comply with the new regulations.

5. Income Needs:

- Reassess your income needs periodically and adjust your withdrawal strategy to ensure you have sufficient funds to cover your expenses.

- Consider the impact of inflation and healthcare costs on your income requirements.

Detailed Example:

- **Scenario:** Lisa, age 75, notices an increase in her healthcare expenses. She adjusts her withdrawal strategy to ensure she has enough income to cover these higher costs.

- **Integration:** She also reviews her healthcare coverage to ensure it meets her needs.

6. **Healthcare and Long-Term Care:**
- Review your healthcare coverage and long-term care insurance policies to ensure they still meet your needs.

- Update your healthcare directives and power of attorney as needed.

Detailed Example:
- **Scenario:** John, age 70, reviews his long-term care insurance policy and healthcare directives.

- **Integration:** He updates his directives to reflect his current wishes and ensures his long-term care policy provides adequate coverage.

Tools and Resources for Staying on Track
1. **Financial Advisor:**
- Work with a financial advisor to review and adjust your plan regularly.

- An advisor can provide expert guidance, help you stay on track, and recommend adjustments based on your changing needs and goals.

Detailed Example:

- **Scenario:** Mary, age 67, works with her financial advisor to conduct an annual review of her retirement plan.

- **Integration:** They assess her goals, review her investment performance, and make necessary adjustments to her strategy.

2. **Retirement Planning Software:**

- Utilize retirement planning software to track your progress, analyze different scenarios, and make informed decisions.

- Many tools offer features such as budgeting, investment tracking, and goal setting.

Detailed Example:

- **Scenario:** Tom, age 65, uses retirement planning software to monitor his portfolio and track his spending.

- **Integration:** The software helps him analyze different scenarios and adjust his withdrawal strategy based on market conditions.

3. **Budgeting Tools:**

- Use budgeting tools to monitor your spending and ensure you are living within your means.

- Regularly update your budget to reflect changes in your income and expenses.

Detailed Example:

- **Scenario:** Susan, age 70, uses a budgeting app to track her monthly expenses and income.

- **Integration:** She updates her budget regularly to reflect changes in her spending and ensures she is living within her means.

4. **Healthcare and Insurance Reviews:**

- Schedule periodic reviews of your healthcare coverage and insurance policies with a professional.

- Ensure you have adequate coverage for your needs and make adjustments as necessary.

Detailed Example:

- **Scenario:** Lisa, age 72, meets with her insurance agent to review her healthcare and long-term care policies.

- **Integration:** They ensure her coverage meets her current needs and make adjustments as necessary.

Case Studies and Examples

Case Study 1: Annual Review and Adjustment

John and Mary, both 70, conduct an annual review of their retirement plan with their financial advisor.

Scenario:

- **Income Needs:** They reassess their income needs and adjust their withdrawal strategy to ensure they have enough funds for the upcoming year.

- **Investment Performance:** Their advisor reviews their portfolio performance and recommends rebalancing to maintain their desired asset allocation.

- **Estate Planning:** John and Mary update their wills and beneficiary designations to reflect changes in their family situation.

Outcome:

- Regular reviews and adjustments help John and Mary stay on track and ensure their retirement plan remains aligned with their goals and needs.

Case Study 2: Responding to Market Volatility

Susan, 68, experiences significant market volatility that impacts her investment portfolio.

Scenario:

- **Portfolio Adjustment:** Susan works with her financial advisor to assess the impact of the market downturn on her portfolio.

- **Rebalancing:** They decide to rebalance her portfolio to reduce risk and maintain her desired asset allocation.

- **Withdrawal Strategy:** Susan adjusts her withdrawal strategy, reducing her withdrawals temporarily to preserve her investments.

Outcome:

- By responding proactively to market conditions, Susan mitigates the impact of volatility on her retirement savings and maintains financial stability.

Case Study 3: Adjusting for Life Events

Tom, 72, recently lost his spouse and needs to adjust his retirement plan to reflect his new circumstances.

Scenario:

- **Income Needs:** Tom reassesses his income needs and adjusts his withdrawal strategy to ensure he has enough funds for his new living situation.

- **Estate Planning:** He updates his will, trust, and beneficiary designations to reflect his new circumstances.

- **Healthcare Coverage:** Tom reviews his healthcare coverage to ensure it meets his needs as a single retiree.

Outcome:

- Tom's proactive adjustments ensure his retirement plan remains relevant and effective, providing financial stability and peace of mind.

Common Mistakes to Avoid

1. **Infrequent Reviews:** Failing to review your plan regularly can result in outdated strategies that no longer align with your goals or circumstances.

   - **Tip:** Conduct annual reviews to ensure your plan remains relevant and effective.

2. **Ignoring Life Events:** Significant life changes can impact your retirement plan. Ensure your plan reflects your current situation and wishes.

   - **Example:** Update your estate planning documents and beneficiary designations after significant life events.

3. **Neglecting Rebalancing:** Not rebalancing your portfolio can lead to unintended risk exposure. Regularly review and adjust your asset allocation.

   - **Tip:** Set a specific threshold (e.g., 5%) for when to rebalance your portfolio.

4. **Overlooking Policy Changes:** Stay informed about changes in laws and regulations that may affect your retirement plan. Adjust your strategy accordingly.

   - **Tip:** Work with a financial advisor to stay updated on policy changes and their impact on your plan.

Visual Aids

Example Chart: Annual Review Checklist

Review Area	Key Actions
Financial Goals	Reassess goals, adjust plans if needed
Investment Performance	Review portfolio, rebalance if necessary
Income Needs	Adjust withdrawal strategy, update budget
Estate Planning	Update wills, trusts, and beneficiary designations
Healthcare and Long-Term Care	Review coverage, update directives
Policy Changes	Stay informed, adjust plan based on new laws

Example Chart: Impact of Life Events on Retirement Plan

Life Event	Key Adjustments
Marriage/Divorce	Update beneficiary designations, reassess goals
Birth of a Child/Grandchild	Update estate plan, consider education funding
Death of a Spouse	Reassess income needs, update estate plan
Significant Health Change	Review healthcare coverage, adjust budget

Example Table: Dynamic Withdrawal Strategy

Year	Market Return	Portfolio Value	Withdrawal Percentage	Withdrawal Amount
1	+10%	$1,000,000	4%	$40,000
2	-10%	$900,000	3%	$27,000

3	+5%	$918,000	4%	$36,720
4	0%	$918,000	4%	$36,720

Conclusion of Chapter 10

Regularly reviewing and adjusting your retirement plan is essential for ensuring it remains aligned with your goals and needs. By conducting annual reviews, responding to life events, adjusting for market conditions, staying informed about policy changes, and reassessing your income needs, you can maintain a relevant and effective plan. Utilize tools and resources such as financial advisors, retirement planning software, and budgeting tools to stay on track and make informed decisions. A proactive approach to reviewing and adjusting your plan provides financial stability, peace of mind, and a clear path to achieving your retirement goals.

CONCLUSION

RECAP OF KEY POINTS

Planning for retirement is a multifaceted process that requires careful consideration of various aspects to ensure financial security and fulfillment. Throughout this book, we have covered critical topics and strategies to help you navigate retirement with confidence:

1. **Maximizing Social Security Benefits:**
   - Understand the importance of timing your claims and explore strategies to optimize your benefits.

2. **Creating a Sustainable Income Plan:**
   - Use the Bucket Plan® approach and dynamic withdrawal strategies to ensure a steady income stream throughout retirement.

3. **Understanding Sequence of Returns Risk:**
   - Recognize the impact of market volatility on your portfolio and implement strategies to mitigate this risk.

4. **Growth Planning and Asset Allocation:**

- Diversify your investments, rebalance your portfolio regularly, and align your asset allocation with your risk tolerance and goals.

5. **Tax Planning for Retirees:**
   - Implement tax-efficient withdrawal strategies, consider Roth conversions, and stay informed about tax laws to minimize your tax burden.

6. **Healthcare and Long-Term Care Planning:**
   - Ensure you have adequate healthcare coverage, plan for potential long-term care needs, and establish healthcare directives.

7. **Estate Planning Essentials:**
   - Create and update key estate planning documents, such as wills and trusts, and ensure your beneficiary designations are current.

8. **Non-Financial Aspects of Retirement:**
   - Focus on finding purpose and fulfillment, building social connections, pursuing hobbies and travel, and engaging in lifelong learning and personal growth.

9. **Integrating All Components into a Cohesive Plan:**
   - Coordinate income, growth, tax, healthcare, and estate planning with personal fulfillment goals to create a comprehensive retirement strategy.

10. Reviewing and Adjusting Your Plan:

- Conduct regular reviews, respond to life events, evaluate market conditions, and stay informed about policy changes to keep your plan relevant and effective.

Encouragement to Take Action

Retirement is a significant life transition that offers both challenges and opportunities. By taking a proactive approach and implementing the strategies outlined in this book, you can create a retirement plan that provides financial security and enhances your overall well-being.

1. Start Planning Early:

- The earlier you start planning for retirement, the more options and flexibility you will have. Begin by assessing your current financial situation, setting goals, and developing a plan.

2. Stay Informed:

- Continuously educate yourself about retirement planning, tax laws, healthcare options, and other relevant topics. Staying informed will help you make better decisions and adapt to changes.

3. Seek Professional Guidance:

- Consider working with a financial advisor, tax professional, or estate planning attorney to ensure your plan is comprehensive and tailored to your needs.

4. **Be Flexible and Adaptable:**

   - Life is unpredictable, and your retirement plan should be flexible enough to adapt to changes in your circumstances, goals, and the economic environment.

5. **Focus on Personal Fulfillment:**

   - Remember that retirement is not just about finances. Prioritize activities and relationships that bring joy and meaning to your life.

Final Thoughts on Achieving a Successful and Fulfilling Retirement

A successful and fulfilling retirement is within your reach. By taking a holistic approach and integrating all aspects of your retirement plan, you can ensure financial security, manage risks, and enjoy a rich and rewarding retirement experience. Embrace this new chapter of your life with confidence, knowing that you have the tools and knowledge to navigate the journey ahead.

APPENDICES

Worksheets and Planning Tools

1. **Retirement Income Planning Worksheet:** A tool to help you calculate your expected income from various sources and plan your withdrawals.

2. **Healthcare and Long-Term Care Planning Checklist:** A checklist to ensure you have considered all aspects of healthcare and long-term care planning.

3. **Estate Planning Document Checklist:** A list of essential estate planning documents and considerations.

4. **Personal Fulfillment Goal Setting Worksheet:** A tool to help you identify and set personal goals for retirement.

Additional Resources and Reading

1. **Books:**
   - "How to Make Your Money Last" by Jane Bryant Quinn
   - "The New Retirementality" by Mitch Anthony
   - "Retirement Reinvention" by Robin Ryan

2. **Websites:**
   - Social Security Administration: www.ssa.gov
   - Medicare: www.medicare.gov

- o AARP: www.aarp.org

3. **Tools and Calculators:**
   - o Retirement Planning Calculators: Available on financial websites such as Vanguard, Fidelity, and Charles Schwab.
   - o Social Security Benefits Calculator: www.ssa.gov/benefits/retirement/estimator.html

Glossary of Key Terms

1. **Annuity:** A financial product that provides a guaranteed income stream, typically used for retirement.

2. **Beneficiary Designation:** A legal document that names the person or entity to receive assets upon the owner's death.

3. **Bucket Plan®:** A retirement income planning strategy that segments assets into different "buckets" based on time horizons.

4. **Estate Planning:** The process of arranging for the management and disposal of a person's estate after death.

5. **Long-Term Care Insurance:** Insurance that covers the cost of long-term care services, such as home care, assisted living, and nursing home care.

6. **Medicare:** The federal health insurance program for people aged 65 and older, as well as some younger individuals with disabilities.

7. **Roth Conversion:** The process of transferring funds from a traditional IRA to a Roth IRA, resulting in tax-free withdrawals in the future.

8. **Sequence of Returns Risk:** The risk that the timing of withdrawals from retirement accounts will negatively impact the overall value of the portfolio.

REFERENCES

1. **Social Security Administration**: For detailed information on Social Security benefits, visit www.ssa.gov.

2. **Medicare**: For comprehensive information on Medicare coverage and enrollment, visit www.medicare.gov.

3. **Internal Revenue Service (IRS)**: For information on tax-advantaged retirement accounts, required minimum distributions (RMDs), and tax planning, visit www.irs.gov.

4. **U.S. Department of Labor**: For information on employer-sponsored retirement plans and fiduciary responsibilities, visit www.dol.gov/agencies/ebsa.

5. **Financial Industry Regulatory Authority (FINRA)**: For information on investment products, risk management, and investor education, visit www.finra.org.

6. **Consumer Financial Protection Bureau (CFPB)**: For resources on managing finances in retirement and avoiding fraud, visit www.consumerfinance.gov.

7. **American Association of Retired Persons (AARP)**: For resources on retirement planning, healthcare, and long-term care, visit www.aarp.org.

8. **National Association of Personal Financial Advisors (NAPFA)**: For information on finding a fee-only financial advisor, visit www.napfa.org.

9. **Certified Financial Planner Board of Standards, Inc. (CFP Board)**: For information on financial planning and finding a certified financial planner, visit www.cfp.net.

10. **Investment Company Institute (ICI)**: For research and statistics on retirement savings and investment products, visit www.ici.org.

11. **Employee Benefit Research Institute (EBRI)**: For research on retirement income security and healthcare benefits, visit www.ebri.org.

12. **Centers for Medicare & Medicaid Services (CMS)**: For detailed guidelines on Medicare coverage, visit www.cms.gov.

13. **Health and Human Services (HHS)**: For information on long-term care options and planning, visit www.hhs.gov.

14. **Securities and Exchange Commission (SEC)**: For investor education resources and information on regulatory actions, visit www.sec.gov.

15. **National Institute on Aging (NIA)**: For information on aging, health, and wellness in retirement, visit www.nia.nih.gov.

16. **Kiplinger**: For articles and resources on retirement planning, tax strategies, and investment advice, visit www.kiplinger.com.

17. **Morningstar**: For investment research, analysis, and tools, visit www.morningstar.com.

18. **Vanguard**: For resources on retirement planning and investment strategies, visit www.vanguard.com.

19. **Fidelity Investments**: For retirement planning tools, calculators, and educational resources, visit www.fidelity.com.

20. **Charles Schwab**: For information on retirement accounts, investment advice, and financial planning, visit www.schwab.com.

60245062R00060